I0475360

OTHER BOOKS BY MISHA HA BAKA

Poetry

CONFESSIONS OF A LONELY MYSTIC small talk

Short Stories

CONFESSIONS OF A LONELY MYSTIC short talk

TWO WOMEN CONTEMPLATING THE NATURE OF THE UNIVERSE

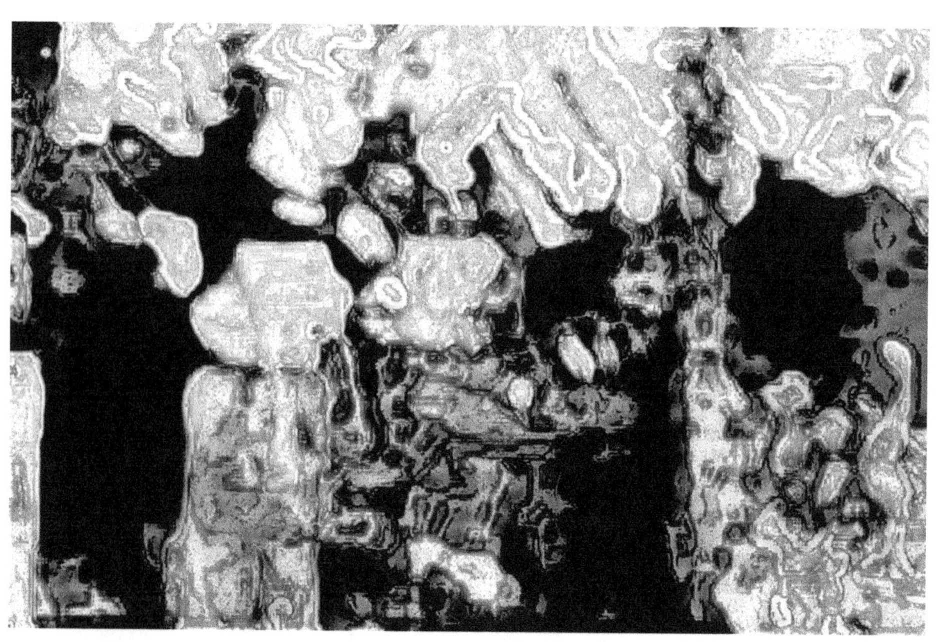

TWO WOMEN CONTEMPLATING THE NATURE OF THE UNIVERSE

PRINT OPERAS BW

BY

MISHA HA BAKA

TWO WOMEN CONTEMPLATING THE NATURE OF THE UNIVERSE Print Operas BW

ISBN-13:978-1543000771
ISBN-10:1543000770

Library of Congress Control Number: 2017902059
CreateSpace Independent Publishing Platform, North Charleston, SC

First edition paperback 2017

Dedication

For The Holy Mother and The Divine Feminine

Print Operas

Two Women Contemplating the Nature of the Universe.................................1

Animus 2

Noah's Ark..3

Journey 4

Gathering...5

Follow the Leader 6

Flight 7

Exodus...8

Sacred Stones 9

Talis Man 10

Escape 11

Assembly 12

Ascent..13

Prophet 14

Caravan 15

Campaign 16

Sermon 17

Knight Herald...18

Crusade..19

Homage 20

Surrender...21

Observers 22

Saucer..23

Still Life 24

Soul Food 25

Index of Print Operas 27

Additional Books by Misha Ha Baka 28

MiKeigh Music 29

As Tiny Tyke, the saga begins 30

About the Artist & Author 32

Operas of the Soul

As a child, I picked up some pastels and began sketching flowers. As a teenager I turned to the camera and started doing photography. At an early age I picked up a guitar and started to compose, or I picked up some brushes and started to paint. Over the years this creativity has manifested itself as photography, music, painting, writing, healing and as of late cooking and baking.

Simultaneous to a driving fascination with ancient philosophies was an attraction to state of the art technologies. I strove to experiment with the innovative technological advances as they came forward. With painting, the medium used always communicated its *intelligence* to me by instructing me how to use it to express both it and myself. Oils taught me fluidity, color, brilliance and longevity; gauche and watercolors taught me patience and precision; Sumi-e taught me speed and tonality; pastels taught me transitional gentleness and ink drawings taught me exactitude and delineation. However, it wasn't until I was able to waltz with the digital camera that I experienced freedom.

The camera was the brush and light was the medium. This light danced across my electronic canvas as I played my inspirational compositions. Then I was faced with the creative choice: How can I take a fluid dancing moment and translate that to a stationary print? After much experimentation, these digital paintings were created. My intent was to produce a print, which stretched the gamut of color intensity and captured the luminosity, brilliance and multi-dimensionality of the original digital art. To this end, I juxtaposed graduated, delineated, linearity against the vibrating, intense, blended color fields to create what I call *Print Operas*.

We art what we are. When I look at the Print Opera series, I can see the technology, the healing energetics, the music, the dance, the luminosity of gems, and the brilliance of metals. All of which echo elements of my experience. It was also much to my surprise when I began to see other things in them too. The seemingly random moments in time and space when synthesized together appeared to whisper and hint at archetypal shapes, dimensional forms and even some stories unfolded. At first I thought that I was creatively fantasizing, but when others, without prompt saw such too, I knew this was not a subjective experience.

Receptive viewers were entranced by the art, as they were absorbed into the Print Opera sequence. They found the experience to be an opportunity of heightened visual excitement coupled with being momentarily transported to a space outside their own. Subsequent viewings were opportunities for a discovery of new aspects which previously were unseen. For me stationary, visual art is a mini-vacation: Like watching a film, you leave your present circumstances and travel elsewhere, even if only for a few moments. The more successful the work, the longer can you stay in it and revisit it over and over again. After having created these works, it was much to my surprise and pleasure to see that so many of the diverse influencing aspects of my life could come together the way they did.

I look at these paintings as synchronistic coincidences, which happen to synergistically integrate to produce archetypal inferences. I see them as being simple, complex, bold, dynamic, and deep. I used whatever state of the art computer, video, and photographic technology available to me to create an encapsulated amalgamation of a dance of light.

These art works are signed and meticulously self-published on fine art paper using gicleé with inks rated high for permanency and are faithfully reproduced in this book. They are also for sale as unsigned reproductions on canvas, on board or on paper.

The creative process was not only a joy to participate in, but it also visually confirmed that there is design inherent in randomness. Perhaps it was the principles of tossing coins to randomly obtain a hexagram in the I Ching, the Chinese Book of Changes that at first inspired me to randomly select images to create the Print Operas. Perhaps it was the mathematical binary exactitude, the basis of computers also inherent within the very same book that gave me the original concept of melding technology with art. In 1982 I was inspired to produce computer generated color art using only a black ink dot matrix printer, an Apple IIe computer and specially self-designed media. Years of working with more traditional mediums and media gave me the foundation to break free and go with the flow of using exact equipment in an in exact manner.

A dream which began in the '70s, that of creating art with music lead me down my path to have a motion/rhythm palette to chose from. I trusted the creative process to allow my art to be a true expression of the diverse influencing aspects of my life. Print Operas in black and white are like moonlit *countryscape*s absent of color, but with gradations and nuances of multifarious shades and textures. They dance and take flight like music, they sing with the highest and lowest ranges of black and white, and they delve and dive deeply into the collective consciousness bringing forth energetic statements of ancient themes with futuristic echoes. They are *Operas of the Soul* or *Print Operas* as I call them. This is the black and white version of the book.

Two Women Contemplating the Nature of the Universe

The first in the series of digital paintings I created was *Two Women Contemplating the Nature of the Universe.* When I looked at it I was surprised to see what appeared to be two figures in the lower left hand corner looking up at the rest of the painting. They looked female. Hence, the "women" part of the title. As to why they were contemplating the nature of the universe? What they were looking at seemed larger than life. It looked elemental and atomic, with gyrating movements of light dancing around against the darkness of space. Of course *they* would be contemplating it since the mind, the heart and the soul attempts to understand what it experiences. For me humor is perhaps one of the greatest healing and transformational art forms that I know. What better way to share these paintings then to have two *wise* females humorously giving their unbridled opinions on what they were looking at?

I hope you enjoy exploring my Operas of the Soul. I hope you enjoy your moments spent with my creativity, and I hope you too contemplate the nature of the universe with a laugh and a smile.

Misha Ha Baka 2017

Two Women Contemplating the Nature of the Universe

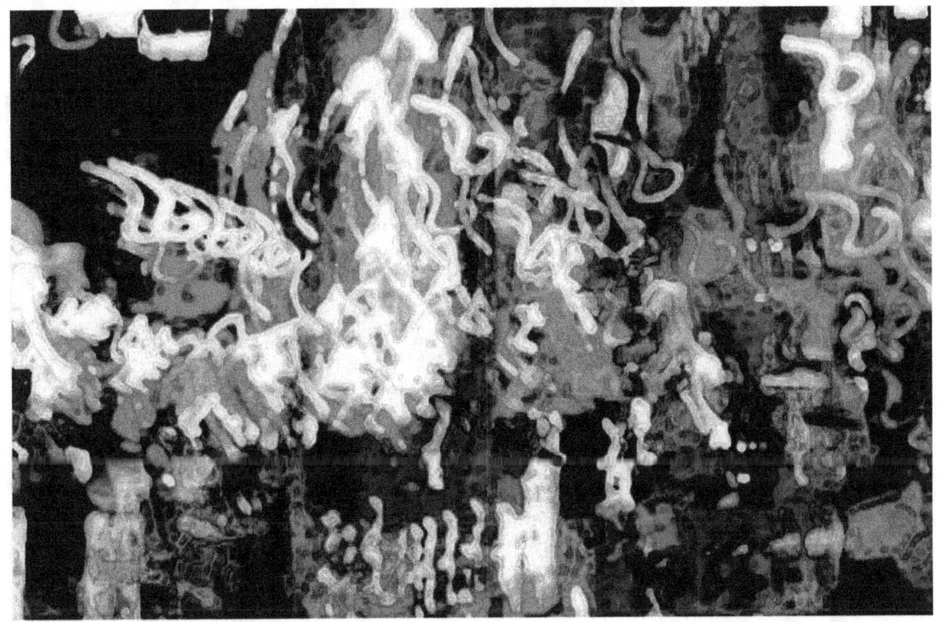

"I think that we should move it a little to the left, right?"
"You are most probably right, but what do we do with what is left?"

Animus

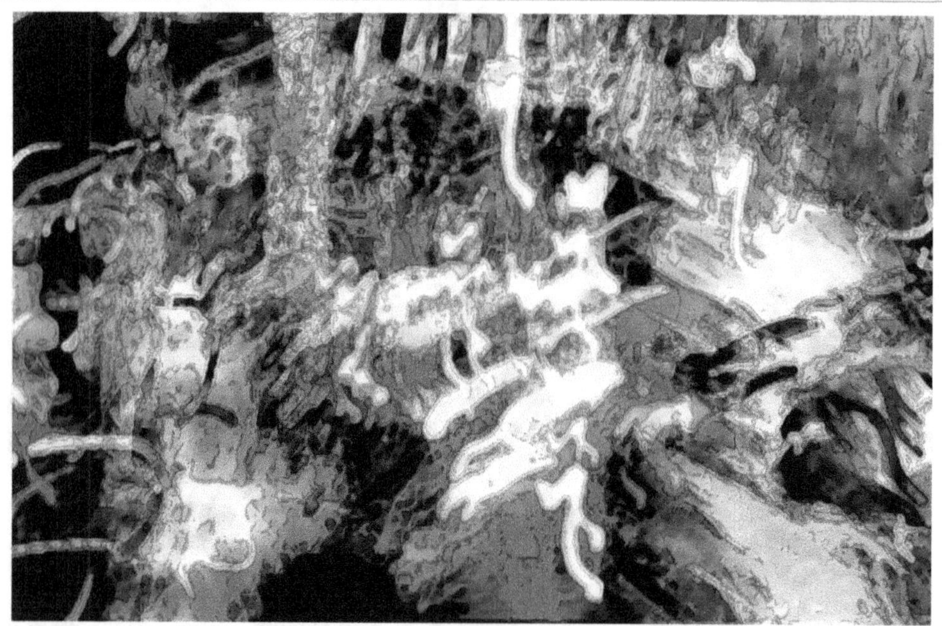

"Perhaps we should put a little of us into all of them?"
"Are you sure it should only be a *little* of us?"

Noah's Ark

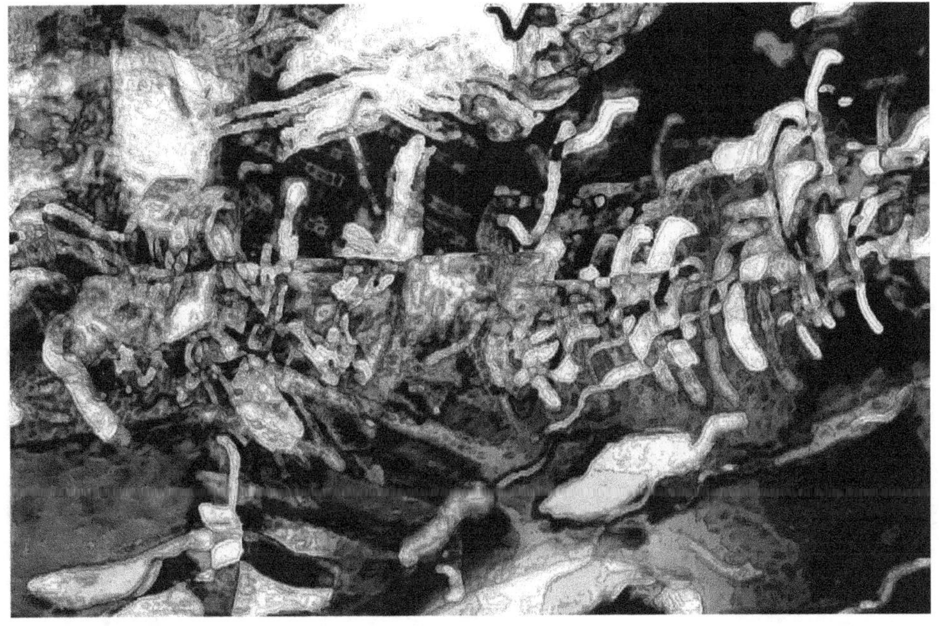

"Good thing that we came along for the ride!"
"Can you imagine where they would be if they forgot to invite us?"

JOURNEY

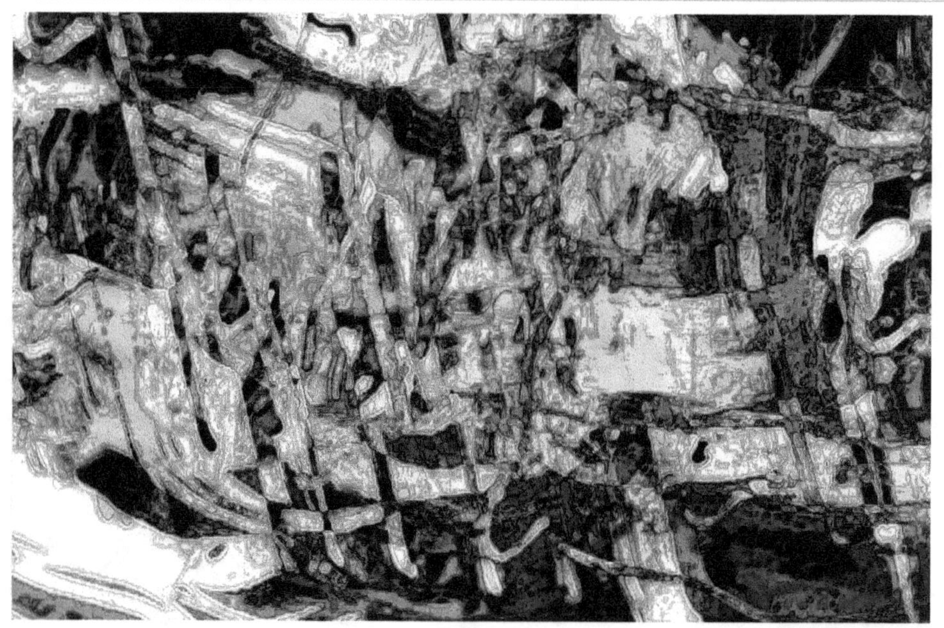

"I thought that I was going to get my own state room for this trip?"
"Are you kidding, we are lucky to be sleeping on some hay."

GATHERING

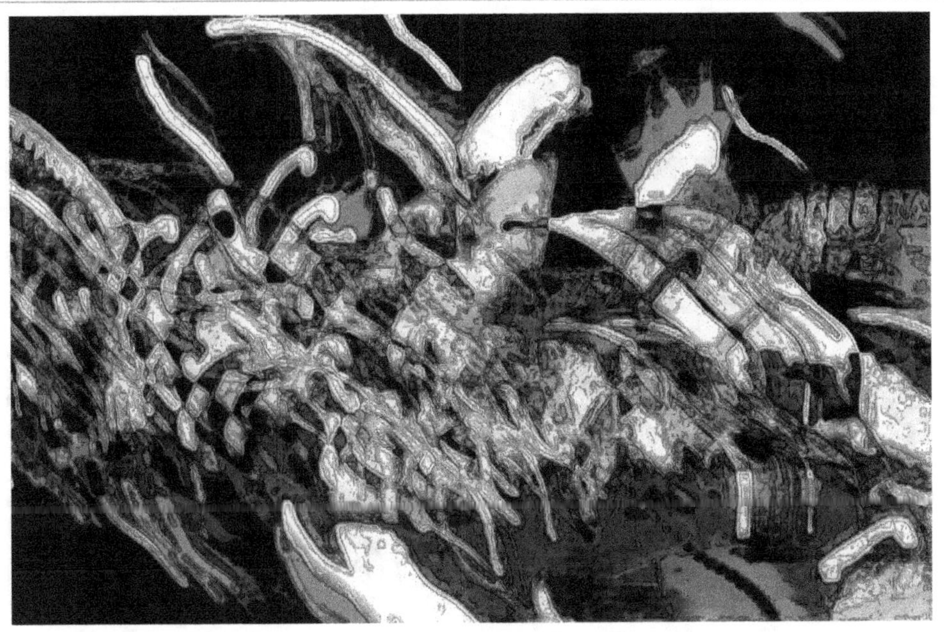

"Why is everybody acting like such a bunch of animals?"
"A good store sale can do that to you."

Follow the Leader

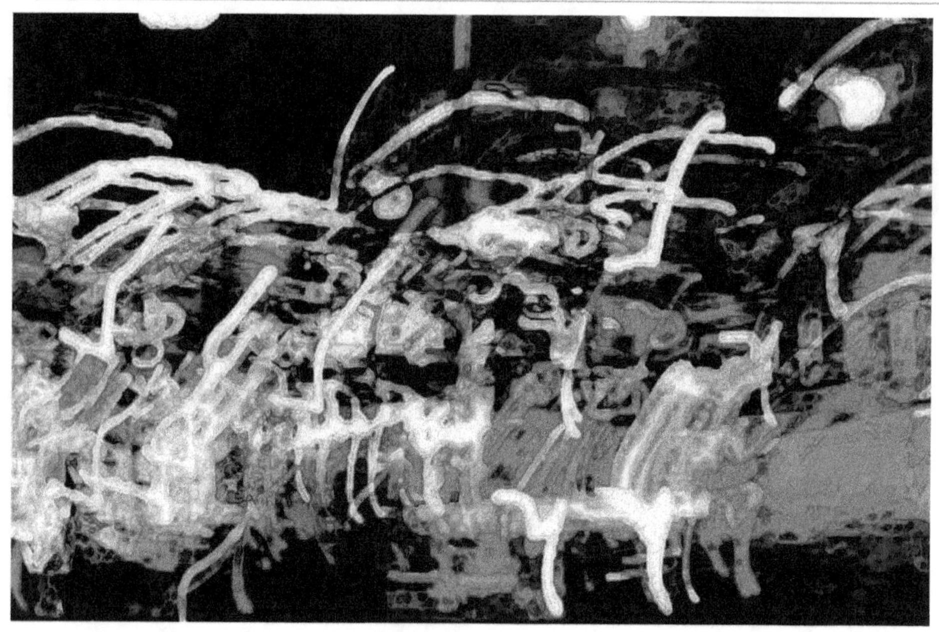

"I said let's make it into a game, not a philosophy."
"We need to be careful, you neva' know who might be listening."

FLIGHT

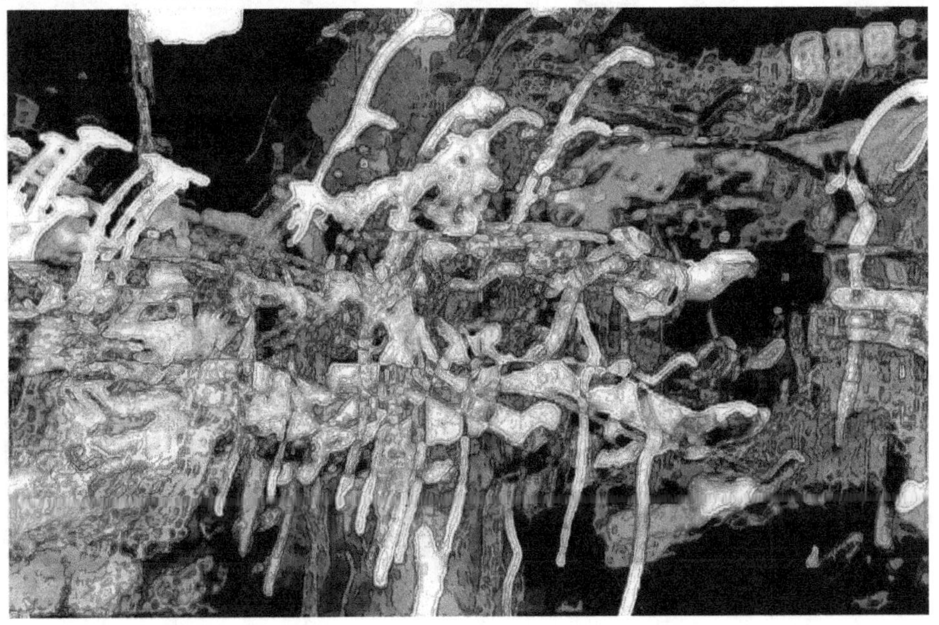

"If I had to leave in as much of a hurry, what would I pack?"
"Essentials: Makeup, handbag, shoes and that special little dress!"

EXODUS

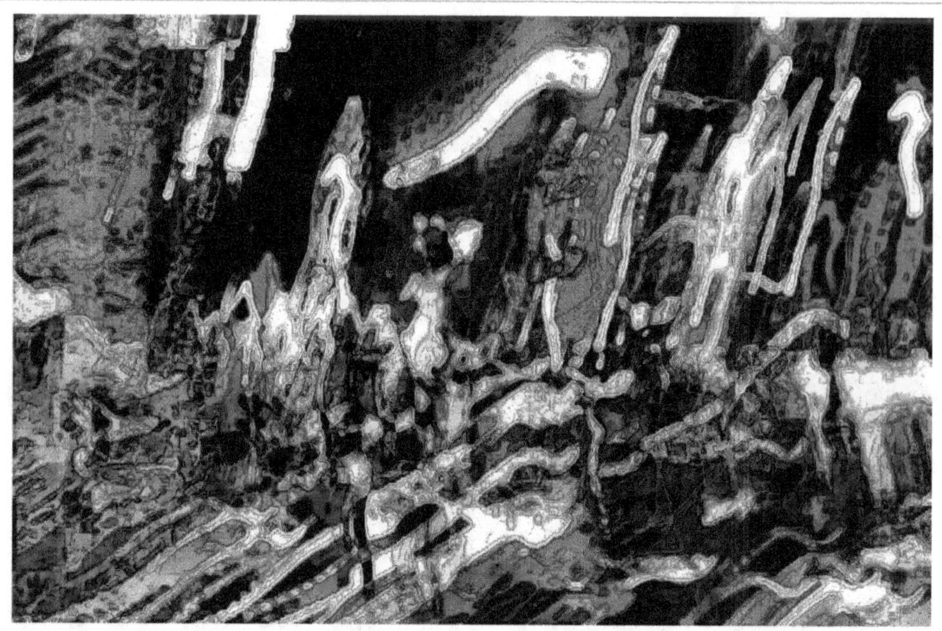

"Somehow I feel like I should pack some snacks?"
"Don't worry; I heard that food will be provided."

SACRED STONES

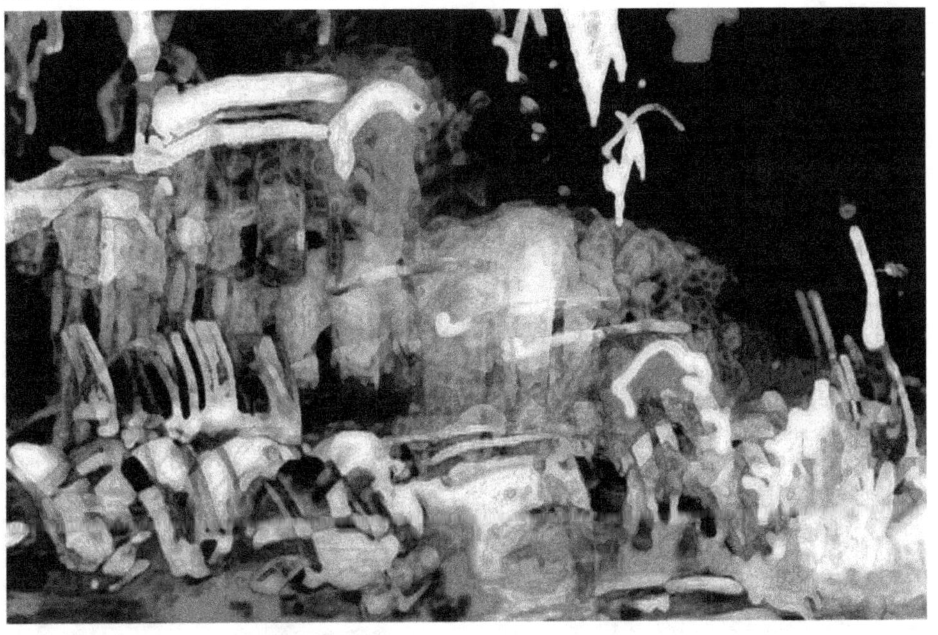

"Can you make out what was written on them?"
"Something about you not being allowed to see Sam again!"

Talis Man

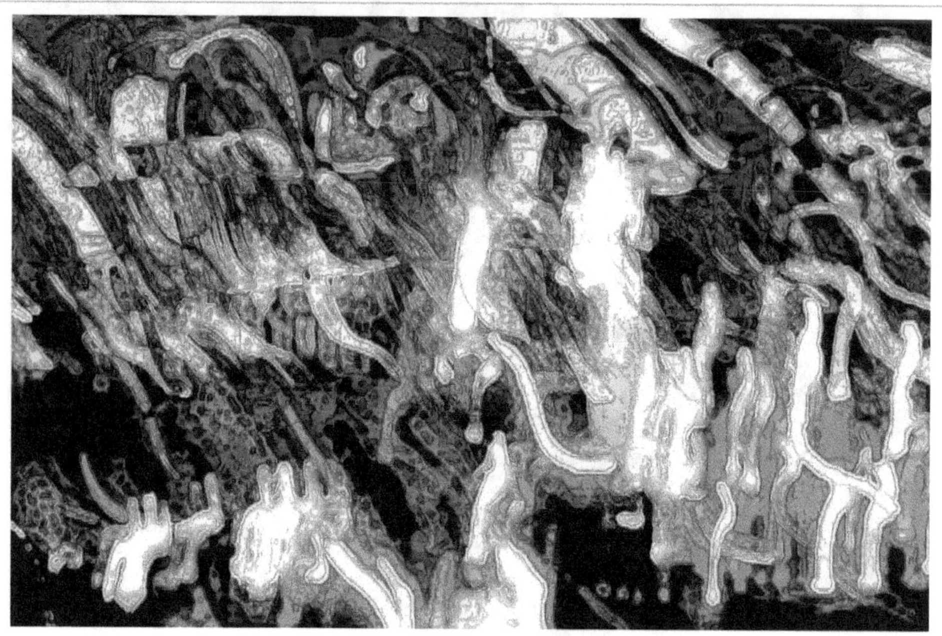

"I can see him standing amongst the multitude."
"Yes, and they are looking up to him."

ESCAPE

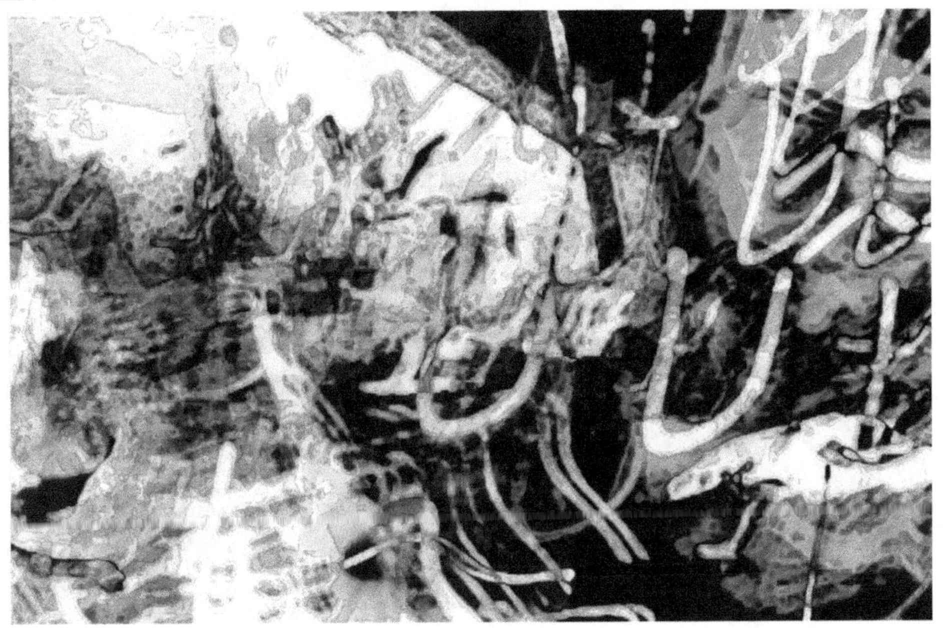

"The path looks clear, but do we have any idea where we are going?"
"Sometimes it's just best to leave the driving to you know *Who*."

Assembly

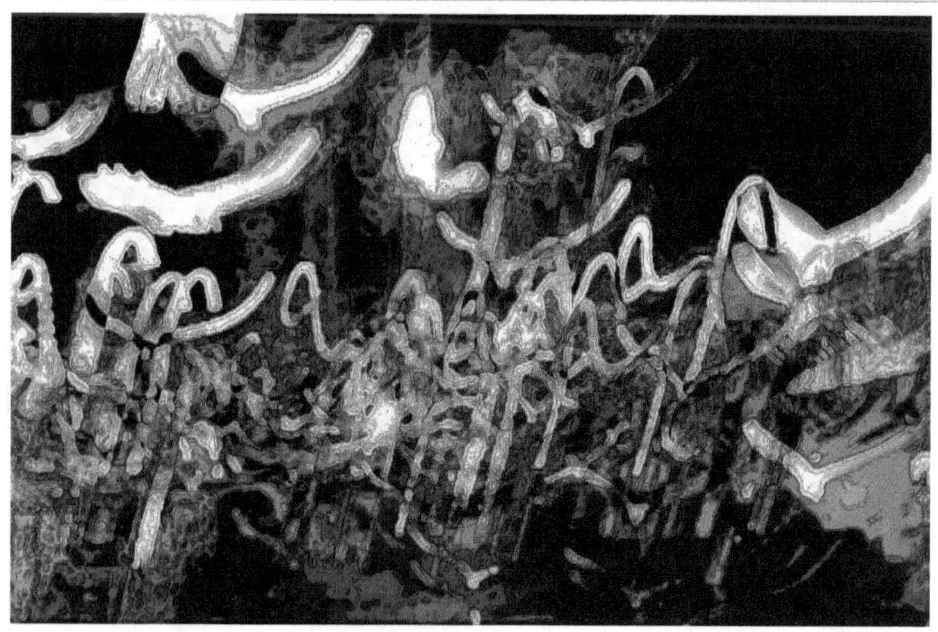

“I hope while we are camped here, it isn’t going to be a long wait.”
“Will they serve double foam, mocha, latte, slow drip, smoothies?”

Ascent

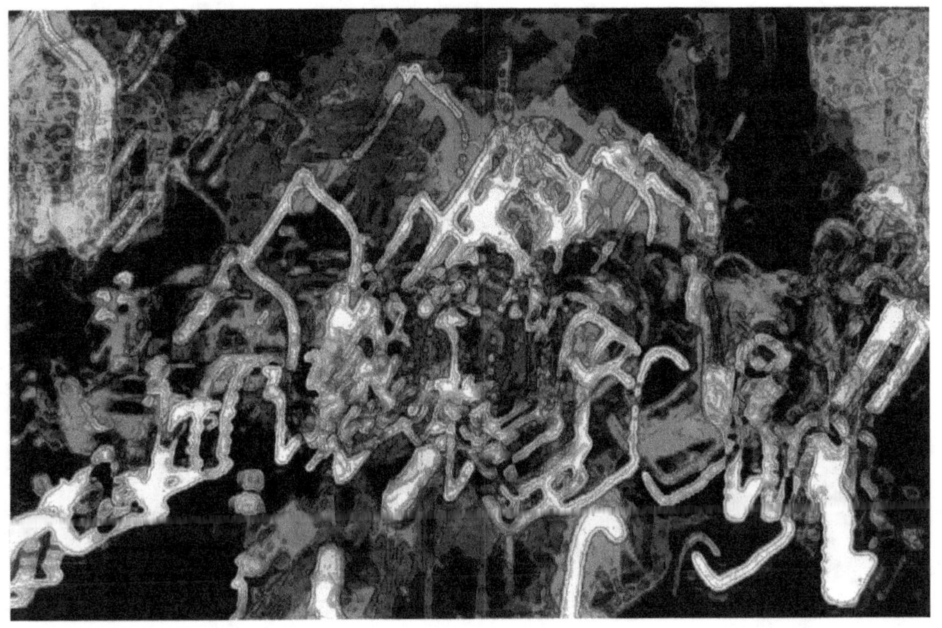

"I'm not wearing the right shoes to climb all the way up there."
"It doesn't matter; your outfit looks great on you anyway."

PROPHET

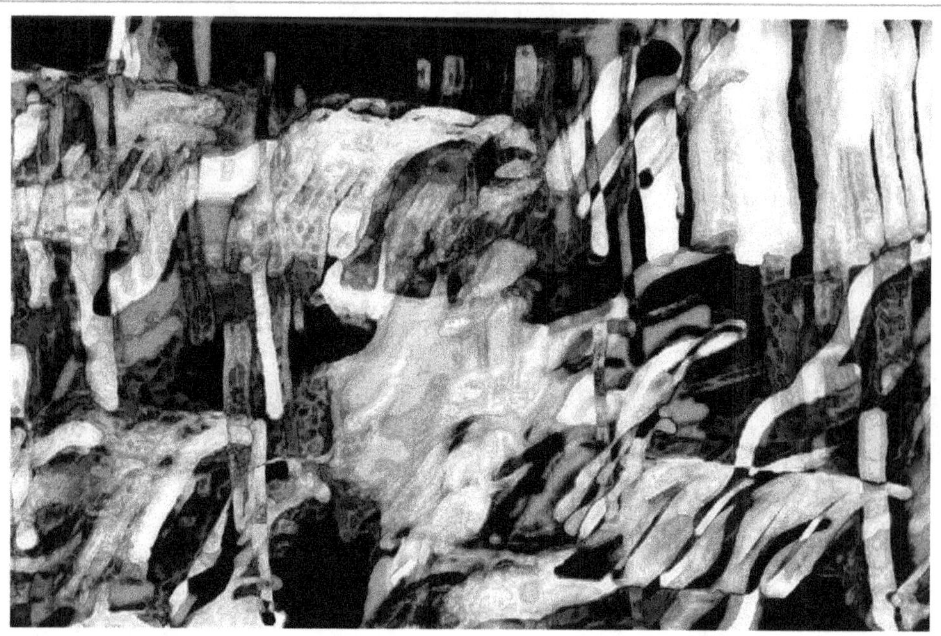

"How come they have always been men?"
"I know, our time will come, and soon I hope."

CARAVAN

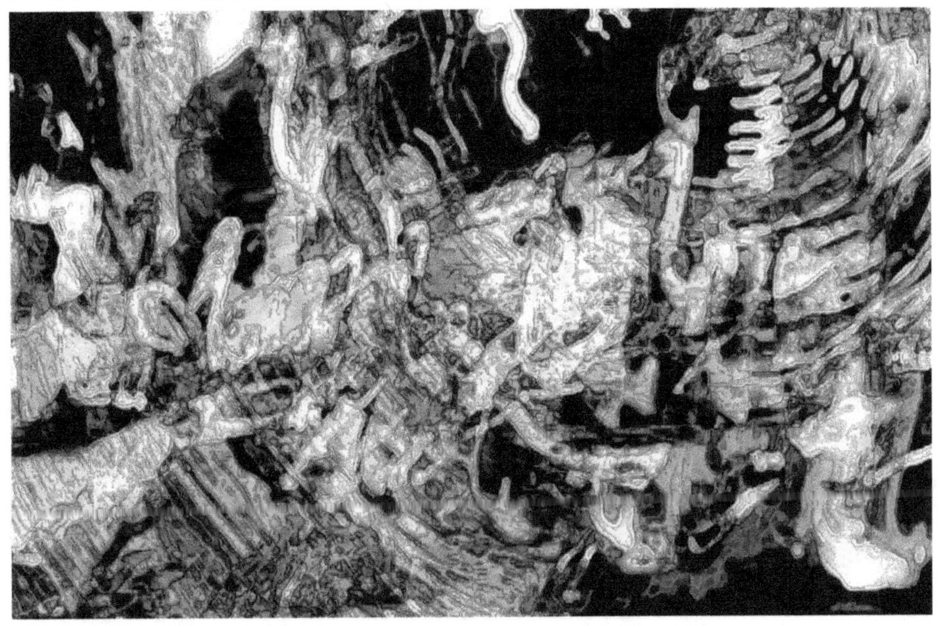

"Did you book us on the camels; I rather not to walk on sand?"
"No, I thought you took care of it; good thing I packed sandals."

CAMPAIGN

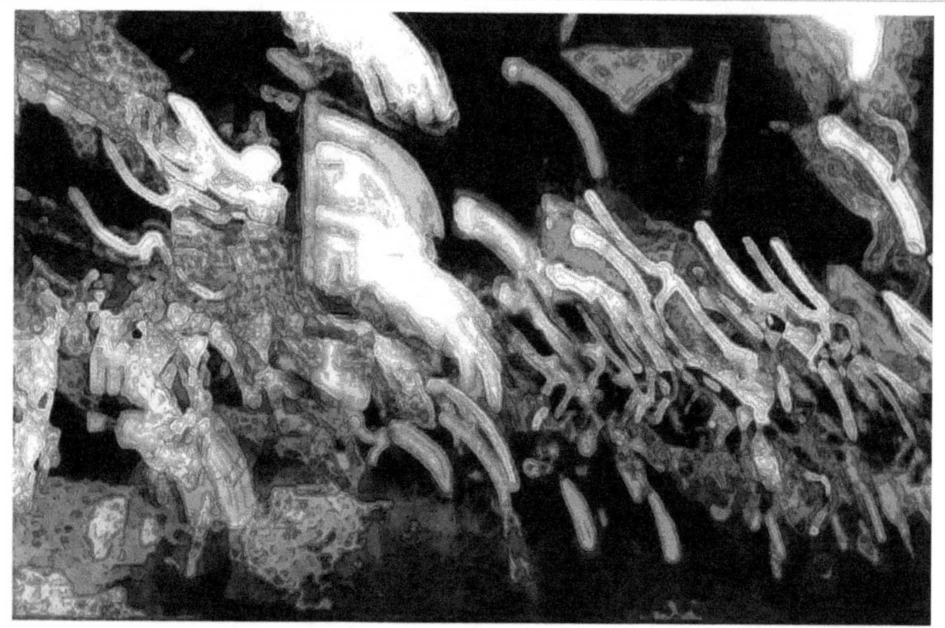

"I'm not sorry that they didn't make us go to war."
"It's the kids, otherwise who knows where we might be."

Sermon

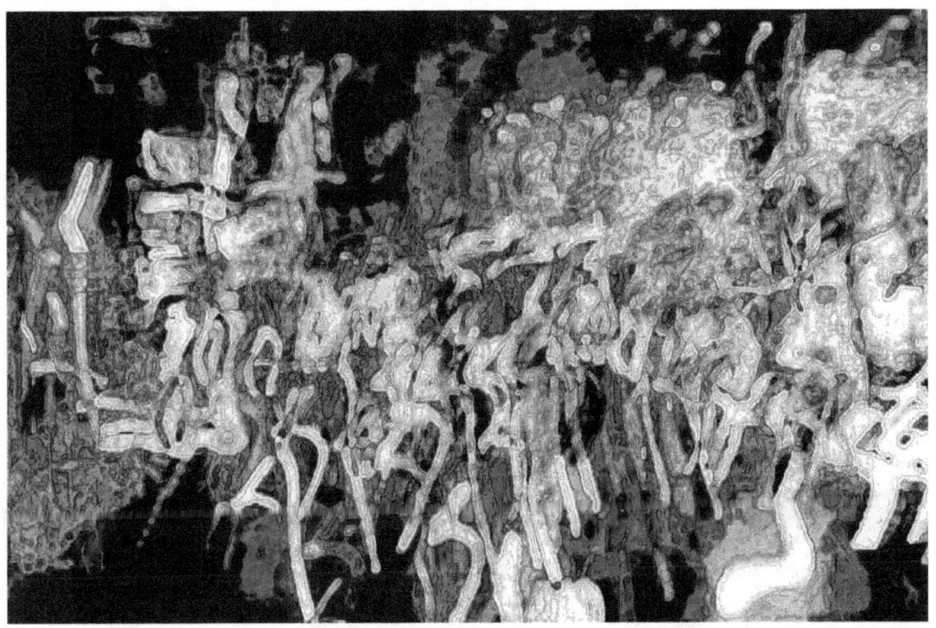

“Don’t you just love the way they interpret everything that was said.”
“It’s a wonder that what was spoken is still somewhere in there.”

Knight Herald

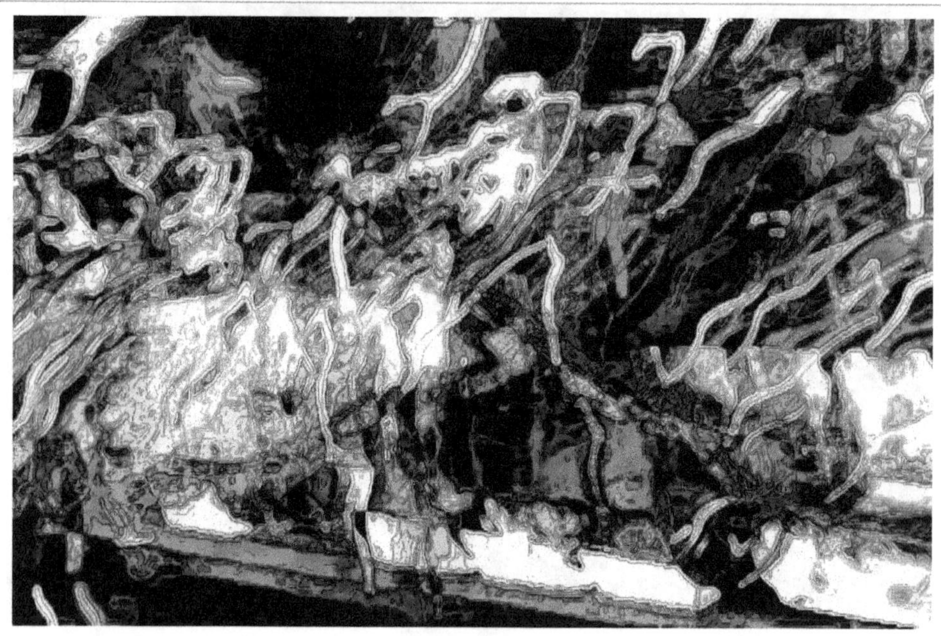

"Those outfits must have weighed a ton."
"Not any more then my hand bag, hat, belt, jewelry and shoes weigh."

CRUSADE

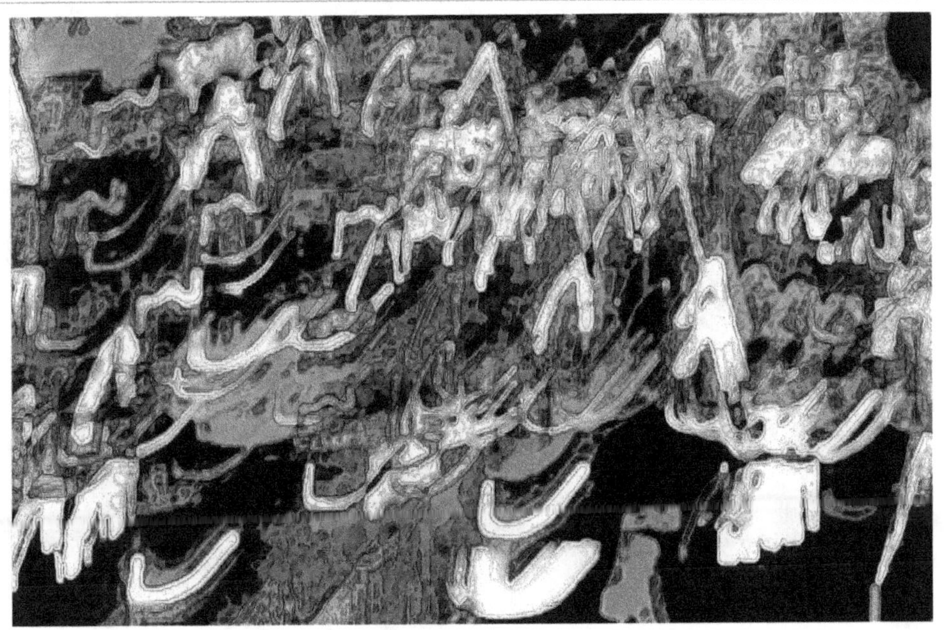

"I'm on a *Crusade* also."
"Searching for a slinky black evening dress is not a *Crusade*."

Homage

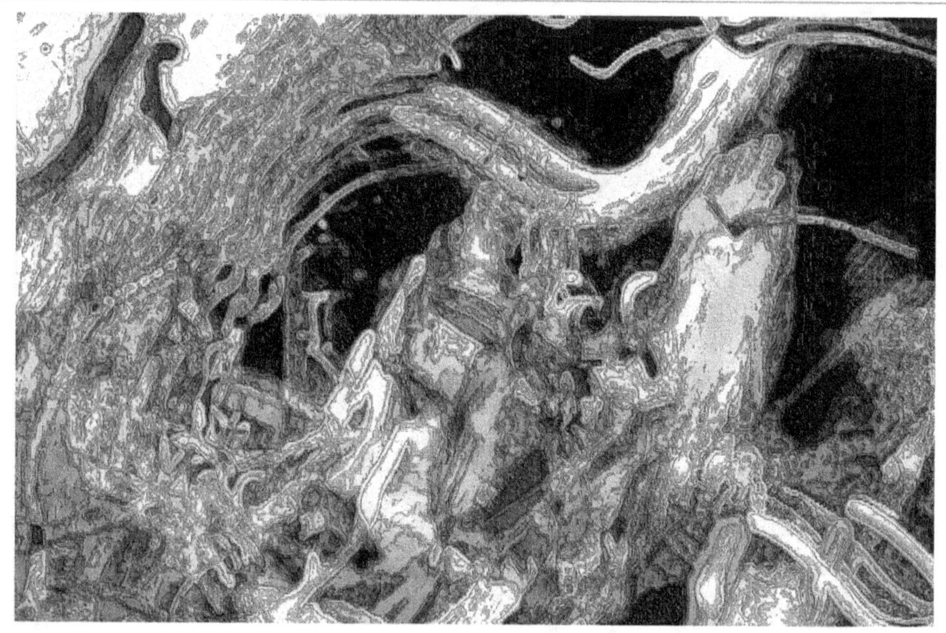

"It's nice to have someone to worship."
"I worshiped Harry until he left me for his neighbor."

SURRENDER

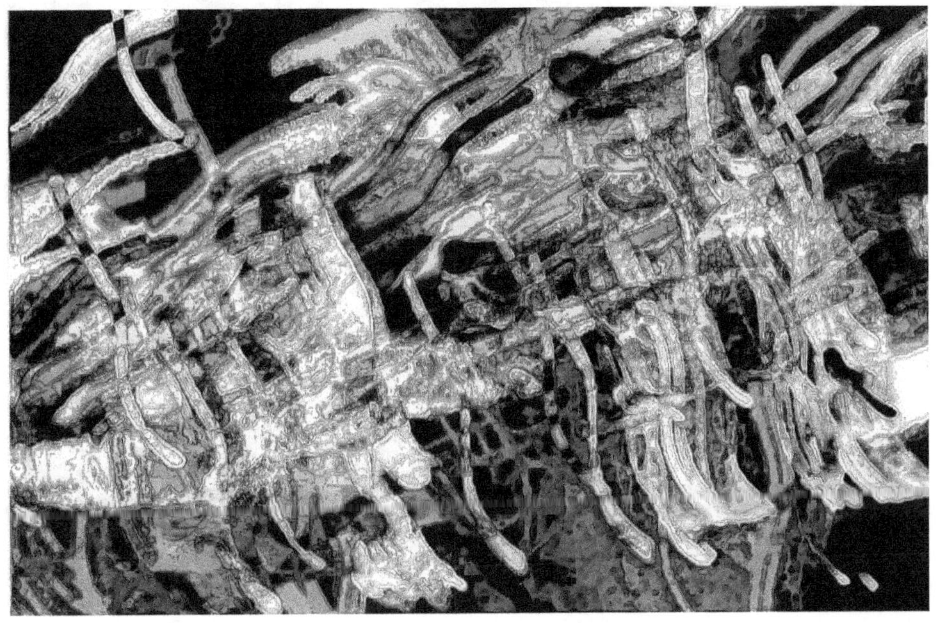

"I surrendered to my Higher Self once, but I wound up gaining weight."
"Eating a pint of ice cream is not considered as surrendering."

OBSERVERS

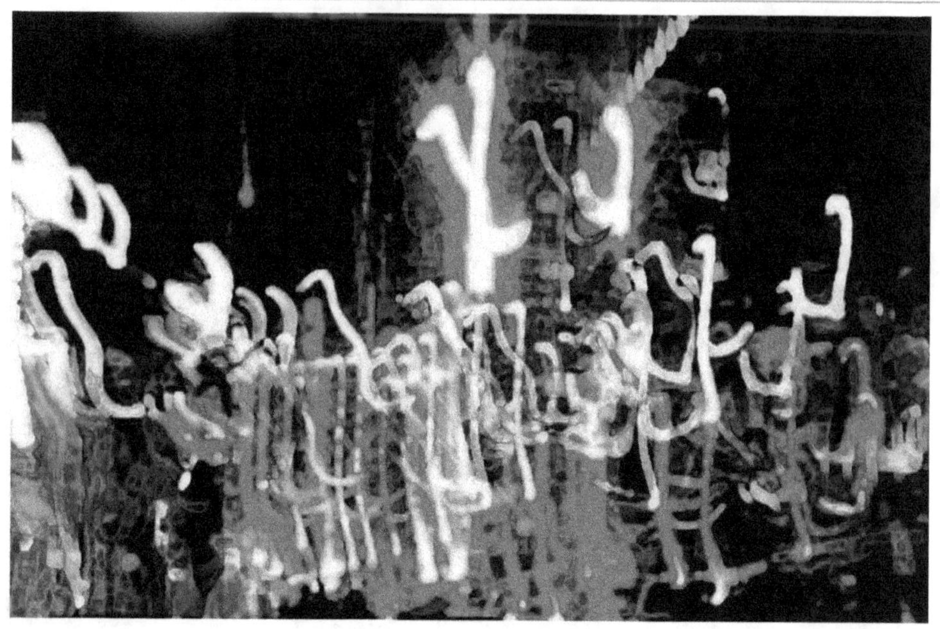

"Do you ever get the feeling that you are being watched?"
"You mean like when I look at myself in the mirror?"

SAUCER

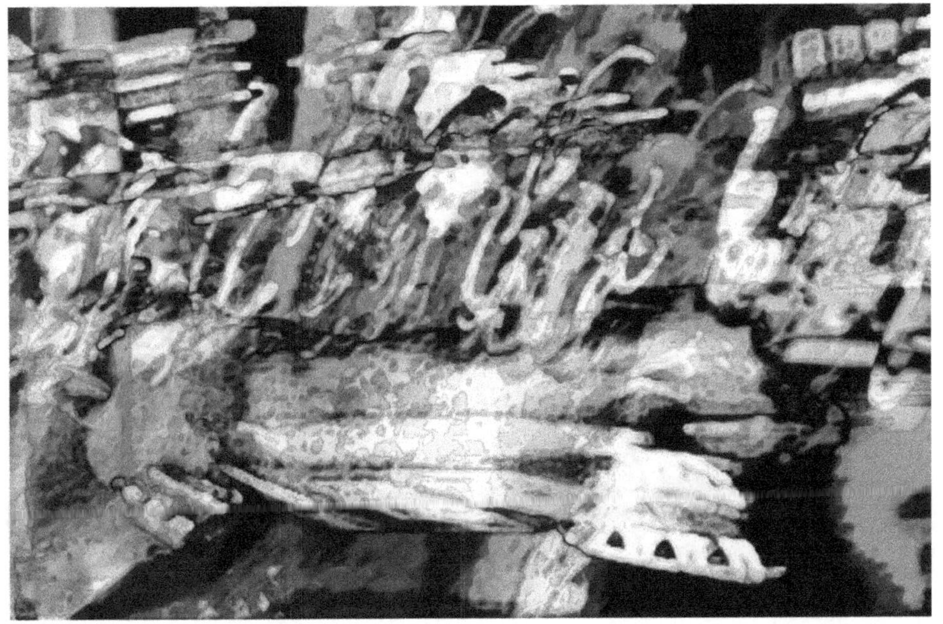

“Do you think they are from another galaxy?”
“If not, then I would have made reservations and eaten there by now."

Still Life

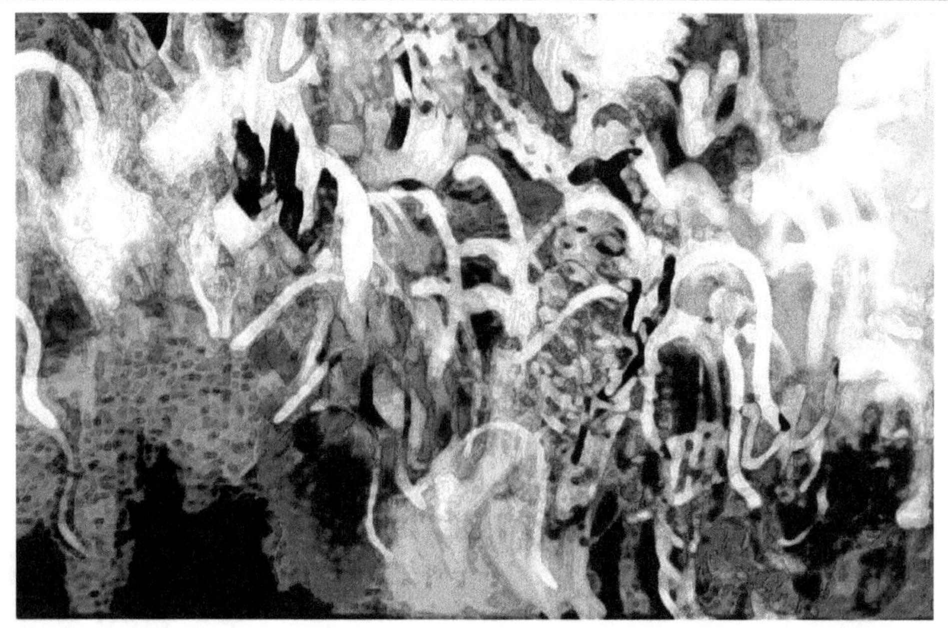

"If it moves, it still has life."
"He still has life, but he's too lazy to move?"

Soul Food

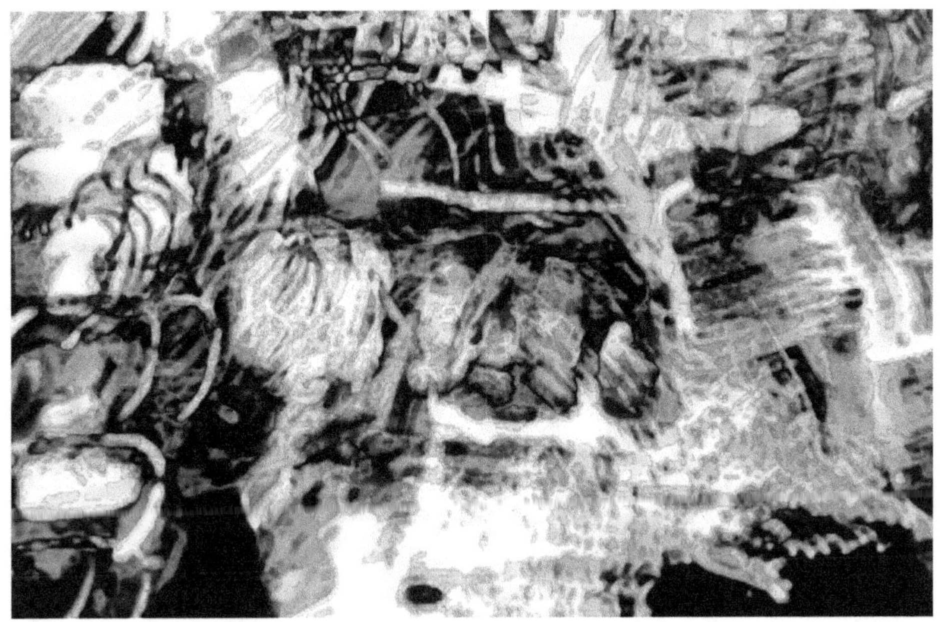

"Did you know that you are what you eat?"
"Do I need to apply for a new passport and visa if I eat takeout?"

Index of Print Operas

Animus, 2
Ascent, 13
Assembly, 12
Campaign, 16
Caravan, 15
Crusade, 19
Escape, 11
Exodus, 8
Flight, 7
Follow the Leader, 6
Gathering, 5
Homage, 20
Journey, 4
Knight Herald, 18
Noah's Ark, 3
Observers, 22
Prophet, 14
Sacred Stones, 9
Saucer, 23
Sermon, 17
Soul Food, 25
Still Life, 24
Surrender, 21
Talis Man, 10
Two Woman Contemplating the Nature of the Universe, 1

Additional Books by Misha Ha Baka

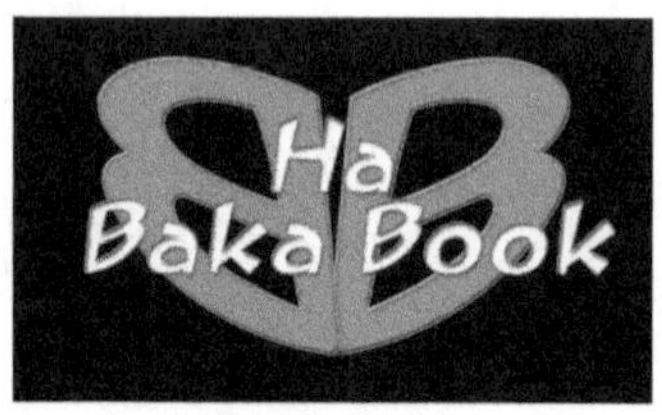

www.habakabook.com

Now that you enjoyed *Two Women Contemplating the Nature of the Universe Print Operas BW* (in black and white), why not see it in vibrant color: *Two Women Contemplating the Nature of the Universe Print Operas*.

Look for the next book in the *Print Opera* series: *Two Woman, Three Flamingoes and a Pooch Print Operas*.

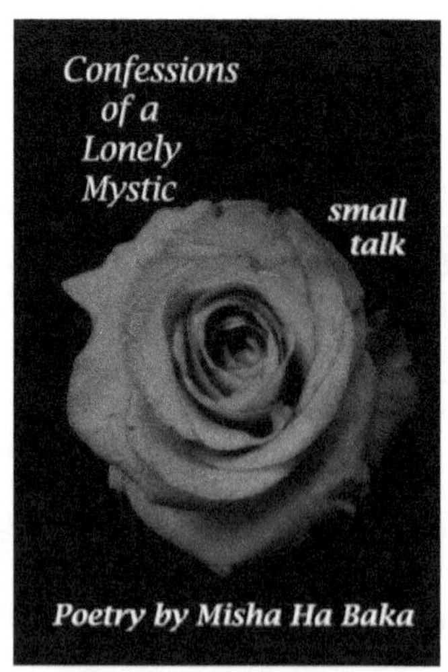

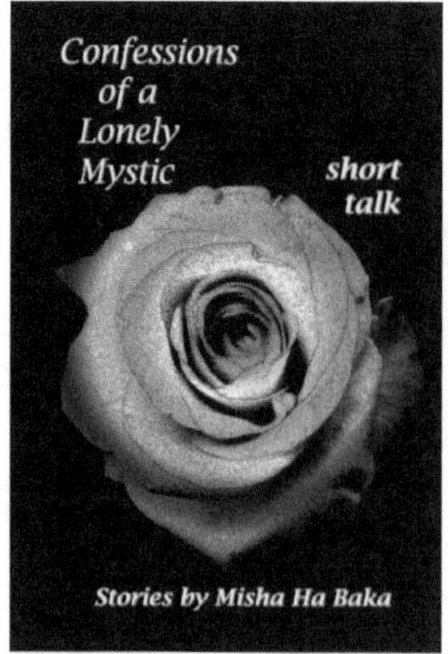

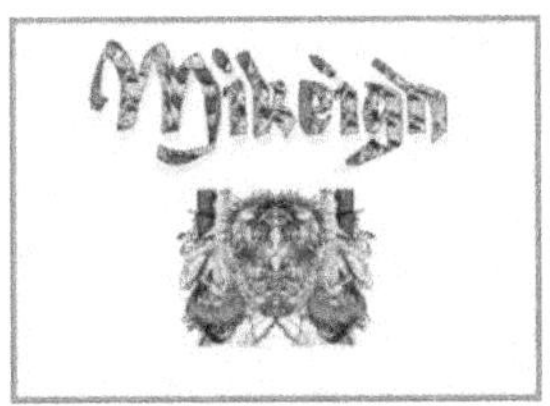

MiKeigh Music

Available for purchase at www.mikeigh.com.

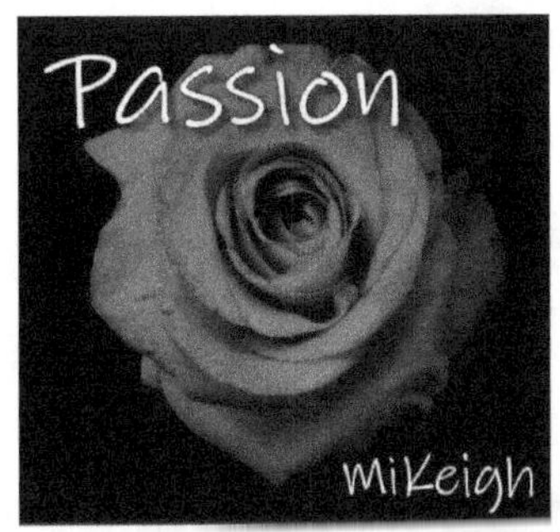

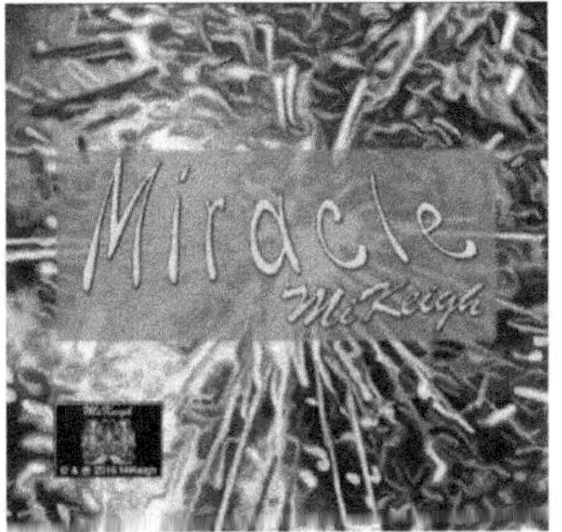

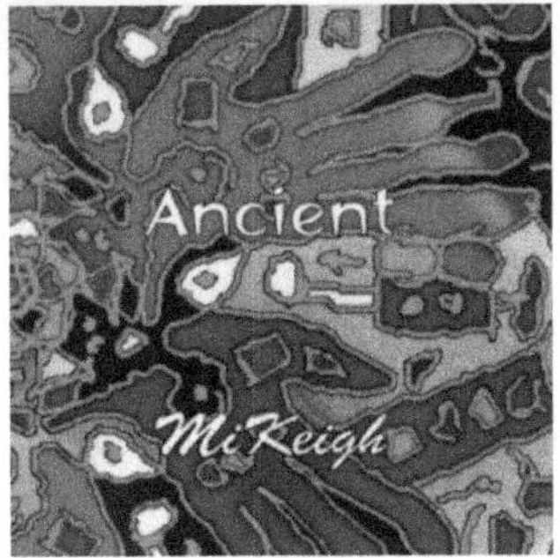

The Lonely Mystic

As Tiny Tyke, the saga begins

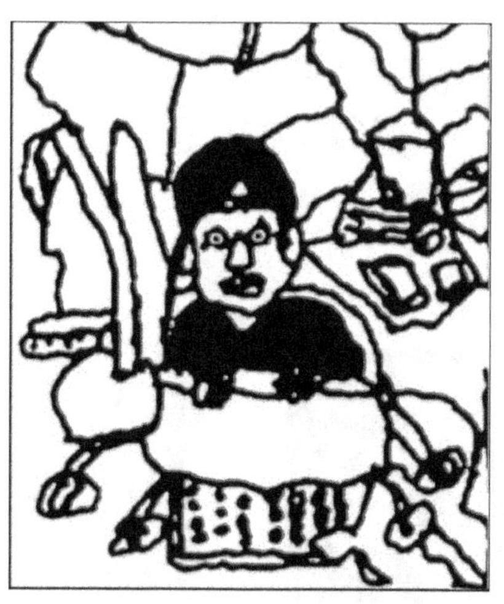

"I'm not in a stroller,

This is a High Roller!"

Excerpted from

Portraits of a Lonely Mystic in 3D

For my beloved wherever she may be…

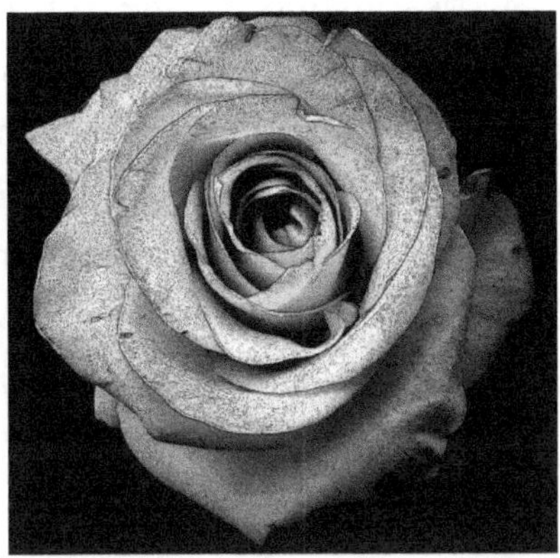

About the Artist & Author

Misha Ha Baka has worn many hats during his professional career. He has penned several other works including the illustrated fictional novels series, Portraits of a Lonely Mystic. He holds a BA in English Literature, a MA in Asian Studies and studied healing and mystic thought in Asia, England, Israel and the United States. He is an ordained spiritual healer and ordained member of the clergy. He is a fine artist, a graphic artist, a photographer, a musician and a composer with dozens of albums of original music such as *Passion*, *Miracle* and *Ancient*.

www.ingramcontent.com/pod-product-compliance
Lightning Source LLC
Chambersburg PA
CBHW071826170526
45167CB00003B/1441

* 9 7 8 1 5 4 3 0 0 0 7 7 1 *